FROM THE MIRY CLAY:

A MEMOIR

GUIDING STEPS TO OVER-COMING OBSTACLES AND ISSUES OF LIFE!

www.lilyinhishands.com

www.bosedeadetunji.com

FROM THE MIRY CLAY:

A MEMOIR

GUIDING STEPS TO OVER-COMING OBSTACLES AND ISSUES OF LIFE!

BOSEDE ADETUNJI

www.lilyinhishands.com

www.bosedeadetunji.com

FROM THE MIRY CLAY:

A MEMOIR!

Guiding Steps to Overcoming Obstacles and Issues of Life

Copyright © 2018 Bosede Adetunji

ISBN- 978-1-7320017-7-0

Printed in The United States of America.

For bulk purchases, please
Please visit: www.lilyinhishands.com
www.bosedeadetunji.com Or
Call: (614) 596-4626

DEDICATION / ACKNOWLEDGEMENTS

In the journey of my life, I met some people; I left some people; I acknowledge all these people, as they are all part of the scenes that make the whole story of my life.

I dedicate this book to Almighty God, the Author of life and destiny changer, for this privilege to see me through the labors and encounters I went through. I believe HE is the Lord of all perfections, and greater things He will yet unwrap in my life in due time in Jesus name.

I also dedicate this to my parents, Pa Elugboyega A. Elujoba JP & Madam Olatundun A. Elujoba JP. You are my vehicles to this planet, and I am eternally grateful for your labor, prayers and supports all through the years. Your unceasing prayers for me and my family are never unnoticed. You are the best parents in this world and I won't trade you for trillions of dollars. Thank you so much.

My sincere dedication is not completed until it is raised for my mother-in-law, Late Madam Victoria Adetunji, whose life was an exemplary for generations to imbibe. The pain of your passing into glory has always been indelible because of your sacrifices of motherhood you paid for the fruits of your loins, but I 'am here to blow the trumpet of your love to the world and your legacy lives on through your children and many. Continue to Rest in Peace 'Maami'. Adieu Mama.

TESTIMONIAL

From the Miry Clay: A Memoir!

A Must Read!

Our lives are stories and our uniqueness makes the story so powerful. I have read thousands of stories over the years but I have never read one that is quite like this. Bosede Adetunji shares from the depths of her heart the amazing journey of struggles, pain, challenges and constant victories she enjoyed from the Author of Life. I recommend this as a veritable tool in the hand of every man and woman of destiny!

– SAMSON KING, Author of *In the Company of the Greats*

A TRUE LIFE GUIDE!

"From The Miry Clay" contains countless examples of learning through life's experiences and completely yielding to God. The testimonies described in this book are real life, raw, and undiluted stories that many can relate to. Sometimes it's hard to see or feel God's love or understand His plan when it seems like your life is filled with trials upon trials. This book is a testament that through it all, "Joy will surely come in the morning..."

I was truly encouraged. I highly recommend reading this book especially if you are in the midst of a difficult life challenge. It will bolster your faith and give you refreshing hope."

~~ **Mrs. 'Damilola Oyeniran, PA, USA.**

TABLE OF CONTENTS

After reading this book, if you feel it has inspired you, I would love to hear from you. You can write an honest review for this book on Amazon. All you need to do is visit www.amazon.com and search for my name or this title. Hopefully, our paths will cross at some point in our lives and we can meet each other in person. I pray that you will be blessed with perfect health, abundant wealth, & never-ending happiness!

You can also visit my website below for more information. God bless you!

BOSEDE ADETUNJI

www.lilyinhishands.com

www.bosedeadetunji.com

INTRODUCTION

This book was put together when the authentic part of me started flaming up, out of its threshold. You want to ask if I was ever mute? No! But I grew up in a culture and conditions that dictated what should be and should not be said. It compounds it, when you are a girl... most girls at my growing up time, don't have to be in some places, don't have to say some things, are not eligible to some standard in education and/or be in some atmosphere, some jobs/professions are not for girls because it will expose them too much, some educational courses, you cannot undertake because it will not make you a future "wife-y" product.

The lists go, on and on. I thank my God, that the era was ending when I came 'on board'. My dad overcame some generational fights, that made education to be his priority, irrespective of his children's gender.

The decision to write this book, came as each tower of life was achieved and after many instances of speaking, counselling and above all, preaching to lives are becoming transformational. I see reactions of "Ha-Ha" and "Whoa" moments on faces, during and after episodes of teaching.

I see cues, both in verbal and non-verbal directions as audience resonated with words and experiences of life I shared or they least expected I would have passed through such situations. So often people called to energize me by asking when they were going to hear or see me through my books. As much as I like books, and I read lots of books (I still have many that are yet to be opened). This led me to use this phase of my transition to put this down in ink and paper before it goes into oblivion.

My purpose of putting this together is to equip readers with substances of life that they can relate with, that is not permanent; and to empower individuals that irrespective of your birth, background, or growing up circumstances, there's no hurdle that cannot be crossed.

Also, to let people know that 'limitations' are mere placards, (if you see it that way) that can easily be blown off with the breath of one's nostrils, rather than allowing it to become a mountain to our destiny.

PREFACE

If I am not mistaken, as I am neither a student nor an intellectual of environmental geography, but I am familiar with clay to be a kind of fine particle soil that is very strong and can be molded to shapes, designs, bricks, ornaments and many artifacts, 'when wet or moistened'. But turned out to be concrete and very strong when it is dry. The effects of the moisture in the clay, make the conversion of 'miry' to be evident.

Miry clay, however, is an environment that can easily be seen to be muddy and sticky, usually in secluded swampy and inside pit areas. My last check on the definition of miry-clay in the Merriam Webster Dictionary says: Miry Clay is:

wet spongy earth; heavy often deep mud or slush; a troublesome or intractable situation.

The above gives us the picture of the features and consistency of miry clay. If this should be related to life experiences and how to identify and cope with getting out from such an environment is what these eulogies are all about. Also, the questions on 'why me in a miry clay' but rather 'how can I get out' of this miry clay will be our focus. Has the writer ever been in any situation that resembles miry clay? What did the writer do to get out? will as well bless your heart.

A man that finds himself in a miry clay environment, is likely going to look dirty and muddy, engulfed with the apprehension of fear (of loneliness and possibly

sinking); will have emotional dis-
turbance, rather pray for a rescuer
to come 'on time'. Standing alone
in such a status is probably not a
solution, the more he struggles
with an attempt to come out, that
is, as he tries to lift a leg to get out,
the other leg is sinking, the efforts
cannot hold the upper body structure, but makes sinking to be emi-
nent; all this muddy/gooey consistency can do is to make him
sink...

Probably the physical part of his
body that can resist sinking more,
if the swinging of his hands can allow his efforts to swim through...
Mind you, this is mud/clay and
not an ocean or sea of water that
enables smooth swimming efforts!
But in Mud/Clay! The degree of
his swinging efforts could make
the situation worse. Mouth too, can

make efforts to scream or shout for help (as loud as he can) and make prayers for rescues to be on sight, if there's any, to be there on time.

Man can fall into miry clay by ignorance, by mistake, unconsciously or because of reward to choices of life. Also, man can fall into the pit of miry clay through circumstances that are above his imaginations, through spiritual warfare and wickedness (if we want to go into spiritual dictates). One can also be in miry clay, if and when God permits season of tests and trials of life. An example was Mr. Job in the bible, the story has it that God permitted Satan to touch and laid his hands-on Job's family, wealth, possessions and his health...

And the Lord said to Satan, "Behold, all that he has is in your power;

only do not lay a hand on his person."
~ *Job 1:12*

Whichever way or mode that may have made man to be in a miry clay, needed a spontaneous remedy, it calls for emergency (in the technology era) and needed immediate help. Otherwise news of memorial will break out.

Miry clay is neither a scenario any man dreams to lay his head, nor circumstances that befit a destiny; you do not wish miry clay experience for someone that is not close to you. When man gets rescued from the miry clay situation, there's often a ha-ha moment of jubilation, rejoicing and sometimes thanksgiving for new life, new chance to live; another phase in one's life and a new opportunity or privilege to live again. So, to say... it is only the living that can praise the Lord... Yes!

What could be the story if rescue does not come 'on time'? It could even be a story of woe to such man, his family, or generation.

This narration resonated with some phases in my life that helped the energy in me to flame up for achieving dreams and all that God has built inside of me. Hence, this is a book containing the story of my rescue from different kinds of miry situations of life, which you, the reader can easily relate with. Few prayer points are provided after each chapter, to help encourage and build readers' faith.

There is no doubt within me that the information on these pages will empower many people to live their purposes, by overcoming obstacles and issues of their life. If I made it above the miry clay, you too CAN!

Chapter 1

HUMILITY BUILDS THE PLATFORM

"With my whole heart, I have sought You; Oh, let me not wander from Your commandments! Your word I have hidden in my heart, That I might not sin against You! ~ Psalms 119:10-11 (NKJV)

I grew to learn quickly at a very tender age, to know what humility entails. While my parents have stories of their Christian background, I grew up in a highly disciplined Christian family. Very God-loving and God-fearing at a tender age. I often imagine all Bible stories. All stories last long in my memories, for days, to an extent of asking questions and wanting to know more of God's words. I knew Biblical stories and their applications at an early age; Praying and fasting was never anything new to me or for me as I grew. I also started having experiences of 'feelings', dreams and still small voices of instruction which I never knew or understood to be evidences of supreme relationships with God.

All along, I was always scared to tell anyone. I better pretend nothing happens, try to forget it or don't tell anyone, in as much as it doesn't harm me; but unknown to me that a part of my brain (long-term memory) was storing the information. At a point, when an event happens and I' am not deterred or surprised, but only to tell my peers "Oh I knew that would happen!" or I will say, "Oh I think

I've been in this situation/environment/or with this or that person before".

This made some of my classmates refused to keep friendship with me, mostly because they are scared of what I will say or what I will see. At a point, I read about the sensitivity called 'Déjà vu'. The story made me to know it was just a sensitivity; this truly relaxed my apprehension. But I couldn't ask the book questions relating to my dreams, visions, soft voices of directions, and many events that literally came to past. These moments of 'Deja-vu' are periods you are either spiritually or physically instructed, through dreams or trance, on things that are about to happen, but you never consider it until it comes to pass. Then you start to remember such encounters or incidents, this is a highest level of scenes of imagination coming into reality.

Wikipedia describes *Déjà vu* as: the phenomenon of having the strong sensation that an event or experience currently being experienced has already been experienced in the past; a feeling of familiarity, and déjà vu (the feeling of having "already lived through" something) is a feeling of recollection.

All I discovered at these times was my uniqueness in my perceptions, deep thinking, trance, dreams and reasoning, which I reveal to colleagues occasionally, but often kept it to myself because I don't want to be alone in my world. One of the hundreds of dreams/trances (or whatever classification it might fall into) during my high school days, was the caving in of a part of the overhead road that joined to my secondary school. My school was situated in a remote village area of Orita-Bashorun in Ibadan.

The last bus terminal was at Bashorun market and we have to get to my school by feet, which was another 2-3 miles away from terminal. Our trekking was always in groups through footpath created in the semi wooded bush road. The road was good for reptiles to occasionally crawl out of their hidden habitats to enjoy some sort of sunshine or cool weather. The construction of the overhead bridge was a big relief and joy for us, believing better days were ahead of us, that would make bus drivers to ply the road soon.

A voice told me, in one of our trekking periods, that a mishap would soon happen to the few months' old bridge, but I never knew how I could relate it to my colleagues, other than telling them "raw"; "as is" way. At least kind of preparing our minds; that we might soon end up with our old footpath trails to school. Statements like, "I foresee this bridge collapsing soon"; "Oh Lord I pray this bridge will not cave in while we are walking on it"; "How are we going to get to school if this bridge falls down? Each time any of these statements was spoken, my classmates always bashed me vehemently with statements like, "Why are you speaking like that?"; "Don't you know people will die if such happens?"; "Are you possessed?"

Alas, there was this faithful early morning of our usual trekking to school, that we met the "road closed" sign, before I could get closer to see the sign, my school mates started making references to my statements. Suddenly, I became a "prophet of doom", this and some other instances made most of my peers refrained from coming closer to me or becoming a close friend.

Also, some parts to be of reference were the dreams about who my husband would be, were revealed to me before we got together. Our relocation to the USA as a family was not a secret to me either, as it came in various forms and panicky spiritual illustrations.

Most or all the dreams were never understood, for I kept most within me or prayed them off because of their scary nature. Examples of some scary dreams I had were: forcing myself from someone's grip to run into an aircraft; had me flying and find myself among white people; had me perched on a dove's back soaring into the sky to drop me in a classroom etc.

Again, I saw myself being helped with my bag by a man in a bid to avoid getting late to an occasion or program, but surprisingly both of us ended up soaring into the sky. I later discovered it was a congregation I had to lead as a Pastor. The reality of being a pastor was dreamt of, as early as my high school days, but became pronounced in my fifth year of wedding. Another dream scene was when a gentle pat on my hand was trying to wake me from an office couch, held a pair of my earrings in his left hand, with a whispered voice, he said, "your husband is here, my work is with him, support him ..." I grew older into spinster-hood before I remembered the ear ring part when it became obvious that God was striking a covenant with me by my ear rings held in his left hand. This was challenged four times, until I decided to do away from ear rings. The man that came on-board after the encounter was the same I thought had been prayed off, came back, after almost 3 years... and the rest, as they say is history!

But when the dreams started to manifest, the understanding started flowing into me that God was granting me grace to peep into my future.

My family background is highly engrossed with series of teachings and lifestyle principles that emphasizes humility to peers, elders, groups, authority, and community. No instruction must be seen as awkward, most especially when it comes from an elderly person. Not only will you carry out the instruction, but with respect and honor (not grudgingly).

Being number one and only girl among my siblings, there's this positional authority that comes with any or all chores I have or to be distributed to my siblings, which they must abide with. It is imperative to know that being #1 and only girl of my family did not guarantee 100% obedience from my brothers. They sometimes gang up against me, re-fuses chores blatantly or opt to go play football (known as soccer in USA) with friends and forfeit their meal or meat, and vice-versa (if that will be their punishment).

But the height of disciplinary measures of my dad (no one will ever believe that now), helped "cut their wings" against my actions or desires. My mom on the other hand, did not believe that house chores are mainly to be done by a girl child. Today all my brothers are excellent when it comes to house chores, cooking, washing, pounding yam (with mortar and pestles), when occasion calls for it, and grinding of stew ingredients with their hands firmly gripping the grinding stones, washing piles of clothe every week was an ap-plauded chore for them all.

These home trainings make us to become an advocate of humility, and abide with instructions in the house, at school or in the community.

I schemed through my young ages without much ado of a trouble shooting child; making lists of easy-going, tender-hearted, very-very clean girl, (and no one messes up my environment with dirt), upholds integrity, always wanted to be of help to my peers. But I developed strong hatred against cheating and seeing people being mistreated or deprived in any form. That is when the lion in me roars to defend people from any injustice. While the lamb in me have no choice than to go into hidden at that point.

The attribute was easily noticed, as many of my peers often logged complaints of someone's actions of deprivation, or someone's pain description to me, and they expected my immediate actions of defense. Not before long in my high school days, I became the "Labor Prefect" even at the lower academic level. Usually you don't get selected for any school position until you are in the final class of high school (back in Africa), except you have academic brilliancy coupled with other factors that are considered. This was a pointer to why I was selected to be the labor prefect of the school for three consecutive years. While I was always picked as the class prefect in each of my high school classes.

Worthy of reference was my extra-curricular activities in my high school days: I used to think that it is a natural process to be part of a track team in one's school. I later thought of many reasons for being 100 meters, 200 meters and 400 meters relay girls, were primarily my size, stature and always want to be a participator at everywhere I found myself, rather than being a spectator. Otherwise my real self detests pains, sprains, fractures or all bodily marks or scars, that is associated to sporting activities.

My academic brilliancy cannot be mentioned without my dad's love and appreciation toward education. He never wanted the struggles he engaged into, before the opportunity to attend high school was given to him, to be repeated in any of his children's life. His struggles of labor and cultivating of farmland, to save money for books and tuition, made him to have deep passion for education. To the glory of Almighty God all his children has a minimum of college degree.

I never knew how he got his 'best in education' strategies. My dad enforced us, especially my immediate brother and myself, into reading. He would buy novels (at least 2), on his way back home from work, especially on Fridays. These had to be read, digested and summarized to him, over the weekend. It took me great efforts to answer the question of "how did dad know what was in the book, when he didn't read with us? All you see is, dad would be nodding his head as we summarize the stories to him. I later found out that he always gets his hints from the back cover of each book ... Hmm! Smart dad!

Readings of these books had to be done before the end of every weekend! Before we knew it, he succeeded in keeping us indoor, no outdoor games except church, no friends except the ones we see/meet at school. Our weekends turned to 'miserable library' sessions. But above all, we (the 2 of us), developed tenacity, competitiveness and hunger to read more. We had boxes of novels, and we would compete in our grammar and vocabulary references.

No book was too big for us to read. On my part, I traded our old ones in exchange for the price of new ones. Eating sweets and cookies became my favorites in lieu of meals. I forgot eating meals most of the time in exchange for reading; my series started with the ones dad bought for us, Pacesetter (I read virtually all books of pacesetter, except the ones our bookseller didn't

know of) until I grew into Mills &
Boons, James Hadley Chase, Har-
old Robins, Chinua Achebe, the ad-
ventures of Gulliver, Sheldon and
host of others. However most of
these books, were read in secret,
not to be seen by dad. He would
tell me that I was too young to
know adult things, so Mills &
Boons was not for me.

James Hadley Chase books are
not for girls, dad will insist. What
do you want to know about hide
and seek and investigative kind of
life? He asks. James Hadley Chase
is all about guns, schemes and
crimes. All these were his insinua-
tions. However, none of our reading times could collide with our
chores and time to be in church.
My parents were very devoted
Christians, believed every word of
scripture, also held men of God

and priests in high esteem. They both had their commitment with the local assembly of Anglican church in our hometown, called St. Philip's Anglican Church, Ayetoro, Ile-Ife, Osun state in Nigeria.

My parents were prominent members of one of the leading associations, known as Ayetoro Improvement League. Their allegiance to the church and their association continued for couple of decades in terms of their donations, fees, annual dues and levies, church association meetings and church anniversaries, despite the distance (almost 100 miles) to where we reside in Ibadan, Oyo State. My family's church membership was of top priority. No late attendance was tolerated. My dad's principle to lateness equals absence. He will classify your lateness to be the same as someone that didn't showed up at all. My dad's name will never be in any late comers' books/register. He would rather be at every appointment minutes earlier than to appear late.

You will not ride in my dad's car if you are yet to be seated in the car prior to him starting the engine. I mean once he's seated behind the steering wheels, the only person that's permitted to touch the car's handle to enter would probably be my mom. He once told me "if you are to meet Jesus for a discussion, that might make Him give you a gift, and you got there 30 mins or 1 hour after the scheduled time, Jesus would have left the venue before your arrival. Mind you Jesus will not leave the gift behind for you to pick it up.... This means you have lost His presence and the gifts attached to His presence" Whoa! was my usual remark. This was the kind of discipline we, the children grew up with. I always feel irritated whenever I see people showing up at an occasion very late and even coming to church late or starting church service/ program late.

We became full members of Christ Apostolic Church, Vineyard of Comfort under the leadership of the founder, Prophet S. K. Abiara at Old Ife road in Ibadan. At my tender age until I left home after I married my husband, we were under the tutelage of this great servant of God. The tutelage of "Baba Abiara", as he is commonly called, makes me to know that the way you lay your bed, you will sleep on it.

Prayer is the water we drink. **Fasting** is our apron string relationship attached to walking in our destiny, and **Praise** is the only link to make God shift HIS base on our behalf. **Giving** is the key to ride on our horse of breakthrough. These 4 major keys embroidered with righteousness through God's words, the Bible, are the teachings "Baba Abiara" drenched us with. Baba, emphatically declared that 'what you are going through are riddles that have answers and decodes in the Bible'. This was the foundation I was privileged to start my life with, which I greatly appreciated, out of which, flows the grace I enjoyed to overcome the appearance of storms, winds and turbulence of life.

Prayers:

- *My Father, My Savior, I continuously declare "all" my foundations to You, and seal them with the concrete of your blood.*
- *My Father, had there been any area of my foundation that has been compromised, Father, repair it NOW in Jesus name.*

Chapter 2

THE ROCK OF GIBRALTAR

He who dwells in the secret place of the Most-High Shall abide under the shadow of the Almighty. I will say of the Lord, "He is my refuge and my fortress; My God, in Him I will trust." - Psalms 91:1-2

Introduction of this chapter is the reason for my strong and unshakable strides, especially at the instance I got out of my parents' loins, to face the dictates of my environment. This also determines the choices I made. Rock is relatively hard, tightly compacted or held together by cement-like minerals, which neither erodes away or breaks into pieces at its exposure to weather conditions.

At researching this rock of Gibraltar, its illustration indicated its top to be round like a cap, drops almost vertically on one side and slopes softly on the other side, very solid and gigantic. This therefore is a symbol of unshakeable, immovable and reliability nature it carries. Metaphorically, the gigantic and unshakeable nature of Almighty God that has been infused into my life, made it possible for me to wade through every phase of all that comes my way. Thus, my feelings and assurance of support and confidence became my pillars.

My corporate experience started at the completion of my course in Mass Communication. I came to be one of the few selected in an employment program designed by the

State government to reduce or eradicate unemployment among graduates. Government's money was granted to some, to start small scale one-man businesses, while someone like me was sent to organizations and companies for an entry level salary job. I was deployed to Broadcasting Corporation of Oyo State (BCOS), Orita-Bashorun, Ibadan. I had my hands full of assignments from creating – planning – recording programs (Kiddie show; Junior Quiz; Your Health) to quickly become a TV producer to 3 major programs.

Hear this beloved, any position you find yourself at every stage of life, never look down on yourself or the assignment, you never can tell what the harvest will bring. Naturally I don't get scared of new things or positions. It wearies me so much to see people, especially in this part of the world to frown or run away from holding or exploring a role in the environment they found themselves. They demean themselves and the gift of God upon their lives. By the time they now recognize to trust God for such responsibility, they will then start to struggle, because they failed to take hold and appreciate the role in the first instance.

This scripture,

> *"And whatever you do, do it heartily, as to the Lord and not to men, knowing that from the Lord you will receive the reward of the inheritance; for you serve the Lord Christ," (Colossians 3:23-24)*

came alive when I was selected to hold a remote but elegant position. I wouldn't know if the reason for the selection was ever related to it being my native land. But the position earned me credibility to be among the first 5 officials in the whole State, with remunerations to back it up.

I became the "local champion" among my rank and file. As the Oyo State representative of Better life for Women in Rural Areas, in the then Ife Central Local Government. I was to take the funds, projects, proposals, goals to enhance the lives of women in villages, country sides and farmlands.

This position enabled me to be the reporter of minutes and events for the Sole Administrator of the local government, and represented the local government at the state and grass-root meeting levels. Even though this role was more of a high in authority, my main execution was to help and be of help to the needy. I devoted so much of my time to supporting and enhancing the lives of these village people, with teachings that further empowered them to develop the needed confidence around their skills. Furthermore, made sure that their expectations and desires at their grass-root level are well represented at the State Government meetings.

I moved around with high levels of confidence at such an early age, money was never a problem for me. There was no office I feared to enter and there was no officer I could not approach.

Intimidation and discouragement were never in my code of reference. All these diligent and tactical approaches to handling assignments, were a great attribute to my selection at my interview as the Assistant Public Relations Officer at Oyo state National Electoral Commission (NEC). The interviewer declared that "you look so young but your curriculum vitae (resume) and recommendations were superb".

Many things seemed perfect for me. I seemed to be the luckiest lady in my generation. My job responsibility required my signing in at my State NEC office, and/or travel to National NEC Headquarters, in Lagos for monthly electoral meetings. Also, to select the number of journalists that would attend state governor's daily briefings for Protocol director's approval, was part of my responsibilities. You see many journalists squirming around me, for them to be selected as one of the Governor's convoy to events, for the day.

My exposure to top rank and file in the state government was so much that I had to be among the governor's convoy to social events. All my official responsibilities never hindered me from serving my God or deterred me from my yearnings to be more like HIM. My roles in my ministerial departments were never compromised. The more I know HIM, the more I want to know HIM. The temptations that comes along with hierarchical positions were never an issue because my school days had baked me hard from having strings of friends.

I relate more platonically and officially with people, than seeking to be liked or to be loved for no reason. My background spiritual teachings formed the basis for my relational attitudes and choice of friends. I knew from outset that I must love all. This is a commandment for me, but I have a mandate to choose right friends, as this is the platform that could either make or break my destiny. Even when friends I took to be 'friend indeed' disappoint me, most of the time, I can only be disappointed ONCE, I quickly trumped into a stronger lady, to put such person into a distrusted group while I move forward. I don't stay too long in pain, because I think the longer I stayed in painful situation, the more I get stuck from either seeing the lessons thereof or moving forward becomes impossible.

Although I might feel lonely, being the only girl in the family and never had strings of acquaintances, but I never felt alone, believing, my companion is always with me.

Above all, my foundational ROCK, (The Rock of Gibraltar) has always been there to show support, to help, to guide and to whisper soothing messages to my heart and hearing.

Prayer:

• *My Father, my Creator, the journey of my life is laid before You, go before me, overtake the crooked ways in my life (my Source, Home, Family, Career) and make it straight.*

Chapter 3

MY RELOCATIONS

(CITY TO CITY)

"Your word is a lamp to my feet and a light to my path" ~ *Psalms 119:110*

Most of the time, when a new page of life is about to be written or opened, trend of movements, shaking, breaking and molding comes into scene. In such moments one either forge forward or break-down. The scripture says that God knows how to relocate His people to the path of their destiny, irrespective of their position or wealth.

I got espoused to my heart throb, thus my relocation to Lagos state of Nigeria. Relocating from my child-

adolescence-adulthood city, Ibadan in Oyo state, was a sporadic
180° turn of my life.

Many of the things being heard
or read became so real. I came to
worlds of reality. Life encounters,
people, environment, life circumstances were the trails I found myself each day. The only sustenance
each day were prayers, scriptures
and my adherence to 'principle
codes'. As earlier indicated, I can
tolerate betrayal once, but the second time will not happen because
I must have learnt one more way of
how I will not again be taken for
granted.

The new environment was very
pathetic for my frail structure to
comprehend. Where I came from,
drivers for taxis and local cabs always make total stop for passengers to enter, or make a back-up

motion of their cab to wherever their passenger stands or alight from their vehicles to help passengers to enter their stopped cab; but this new city, passengers must mile around, sometimes in hundredths to await their buses, to be alerted by the screaming and chanting of the approaching roads, by bus conductors. Above all, to be ready for a running/rushing exercises to meet up with bus, the fastest runner you are, the better. "Lagosian" are known for their loudness and aggressive body-language responses. Discussions among 3 or 4 people sometimes look like an argument or momentary fighting, but it's just a way to drive home a point or a system norm. Lagos without yelling, loudness and blaring of horns is more of a graveyard.

Thus, going out or choosing

friends became more and more stressful for me. All my efforts to make my husband see reason(s) for us to leave Lagos, always became bitter pill which he was never ready to swallow. When I finally settled down to fate, I discovered I became more confident and stronger; I swam through thick forests in my ocean of life that baked me to who I am, even when I am yet arriving at my destination, I am definite, that I have left where I was.

Living in a house filled with other 8 – 10 tenants, was an extreme lifestyle I never bargained for. These experiences were the types I read in books or watched on TV dramas. A house that is deprived of privacy and space. The only space you could boast of is your bedroom. I could only boast of our 2 rooms, commonly known as room and parlor. A typical house where you have to be on a queue to have your morning bath; after which you hastily move out of the bathroom in towel wrapped wet body to finish crème application and dressing, in your one rented room.

While the whole house is subject to one or two pit (short-put) toilet, your area or side of kitchen is designated with wooden "chest cupboard" to keep your kitchen utilities and sometimes your cooking mobile kerosene stove. Otherwise the fuel may be secretly used by other tenants for their food at midnight or drained for their later usage.

Usually, gossip, backbiting, jealousy and other moral menace were the order of the day in this environment on daily basis. You don't need a gate fee for mouths of most women to open to run gossip documentary and life history of other tenant. Education and better lifestyle was never recognized or respected in this environment. Anyway, the point remains that if someone like me, was better than them, why can't I afford better housing than lurking around with them.

Trust me, I (my family) was always their daily topic! The major problem varied with daily perception and mindsets. Everybody, I mean everybody, took me to be very proud, because I don't sit around to mingle or gossip. I don't enter their rooms for no reason, and if I do, I don't sit down, talk less of allowing them to offer me anything. To worsen most of their problem, I don't give anyone the chance to my room; more so, my room area was located at the upstairs, shared with the landlord.

Not only do they have problems to penetrate me, I never allowed my daughter to mix with other kids. The only time neighbors or tenants see my daughter then, was either when I walked her to school or going to church, which we normally trekked. Anytime my daughter is outdoor, you see me too watching with my eagle eyes. The only sets of people that had access to my area room did so through my husband (whom everybody knew before we got married to each other), to keep him company and do the men thing - to discuss politics, newspaper articles, soccer events or listening to news until the bar lines of TV comes up, on TV screen, after the last news for the day "news cap".

Little did anyone know who I was, or where I was coming from. The journey of destiny that took me to a sharp detour of teachings, mingling with issues, tragedies of who people could turn out to be. I never lost focus on the Owner of my life, and never got derailed from trusting God for a turn around. This took me several years of miry experiences, that today shaped me to know much on human relation, I became tough skinned lady with people's action and reaction, but cannot be embittered to relate with them. I only learn one more way on the extent of my relation.

But one thing is sure, God never forsakes His own; whether you are going through tests of life or just walking the manuscript of your destiny, His assurance is:

"Let your conduct be without covetousness; be content with such things as you have. For He Himself has said, "I will never leave you nor forsake you" (Hebrew 13:5)

One of the major reasons we get wearied out and eventually throwin the towel is our haphazard relationship with God. We are His, we are his clay, He is our Potter. He knows us inside out and His thoughts towards us are always thoughts of good and not of evil:

"For I know the thoughts that I think toward you, says the Lord, thoughts of peace and not of evil, to give you a future and a hope"

~~ Jeremiah 29:11

He knows us more than we know ourselves. More importantly

He never promised a world void of tribulations. Unfortunately, we relate with Him as an emergency 9-1-1 and as drive through God, that we call only in times of trouble. For most of the miry detours I drove through, the scripture is my engine oil that kept me going:

"When you pass through the waters, I will be with you; And through the rivers, they shall not overflow you. When you walk through the fire, you shall not be burned, Nor shall the flame scorch you" ~ Isaiah 43:2

Worthy of reference of our typical residence' attribute was some landlord-tenant greedy lifestyle of selling of water to the tenants! All tenants must pay a fee before you can fetch buckets of water; you buy water for your household use, and buy it to wash the bathrooms, toilets and draining gutters, which was routinely washed by all women. Not only that, you MUST also patronize landlady's merchandise; and there was never a time you'll willingly be given back the remaining change after your purchase. As if other tenants' problems were not enough, the landlord's miser way encroached into making life miserable for tenants. Unfortunately, all efforts to move out of the house always got thwarted at our two times attempts. It was then obvious to me that it will take the spiritual hand of God to get us out of the house.

One day, the Holy Ghost annoyance wells up from my inside against all these wicked acts, and prayer and fasting gave me solutions. I decided to stop patronizing ALL merchandise been sold by the landlady in the house, which was totally against the norms of the residents. I had to start to go to another house, farther from ours along the road to fetch my water, free.

The landlady confronted me, abusively with anger, she grew treacherous, wild and very loud about my action:

"You this ...... (called me names), what do you take yourself to be?"

I replied, "Whatever you use your mouth to call me will not stand! All I know is I earned my money, I can buy whatever I like with it, and buy it at anywhere I like. Your chain is broken..."

"Yeh... you called me a witch?" She screamed at me

I retreated and roared back at her, "you say it out already!"

"I will show you that ... o kere si nomba, ki lo gb'oju le?" She said to me *(meaning you are too small, to whom do you belong and wherein lies your confidence?)*

I retorted sharply "The day you attempt to swallow a razor blade, will mark your end on this earth, my backbone is the Mighty man in battle..."

Before I could realize whom, I had engaged with, at the battle front, the whole road was already filled with bystanders.

Oh my God! Was my next thought. What will my husband do when he hears what happened? Will he support me? What will be the outcome if we are evicted? My heart was pounding and beating hard, sweating as if I was in a tenacious weight lifting exercise. I ran into my room, went on my kneel with tears, and wrapped myself around my daughter. I started praying and dipping my entire world into the blood of the Lamb. I became a child who, after a misconduct thought his dad will beat him, then saw the outstretched hands of his dad with smile on his face acknowledging him "you've done so well"

After this public exchange of confrontation, the landlady became a bit friendly, but I didn't give in for her tricks. An astonishing part of it was that, some of the tenants, like 5 of the women, ran along toward me while I was furiously going to my room to pray, were thanking me for my brave heart and confidence to confront the landlady. Unknown to them that my heart was racing like a horse power engine.

I knew it was never going to be physically easy or funny, the extent of these physical and spiritual battle brought me to become a more prayer-FULL and tenacious fasting machine. I lost count of my fasting days and months.

To the glory of Almighty God, I was the first tenant that didn't pay for water again; first to stop washing drainage gutters of the house, I contracted it to someone to come in and wash when it was my turn; the first to stop attending their Ramadan ceremony (because as a tenant, you have to be around, among others to cook the cow, usually slaughtered by the landlord for this occasion); first to reject their Ramadan meat, (one or two others will take the meat and trash it, but I told her not to bring it to my door again, because I will not trash, I don't like wastage, I rather let her know I don't eat or want their meat); to the glory of God, I am the only woman that did not lose marriage nor child in that house.

Other tenants had history of loss of marriage; loss of business; loss of child, loss of spouse, some became pauper to be at the mercy of the landlord before they could put food on their tables. All praise goes back to Almighty God, whose faithfulness is everlasting, His word is Yea and Amen:

"Those who do wickedly against the covenant he shall corrupt with flattery; but the people who know their God shall be strong, and carry out great exploits." ~ Daniel 11:32

Prayers:

- *My Father, my creator, grant me the blanket of grace to continually seek and know you, in each phase of my life's journey*
- *My Father, my Lord, let your blood speak for me and my family, each time I call on your name.*

Chapter 4

PREPARING FOR THE

UNKNOWN

"Are not two sparrows sold for a copper coin? And not one of them falls to the ground apart from your Father's will. But the very hairs of your head are all numbered. Do not fear therefore; you are of more value than many sparrows"

~ Matthew 10:29-31

The entire chapter of Matthew 10 is always a fountain that wells up inside of me each time I am faced with scenario that required my action/decision or intervention. It is an anchor of strength and the cord that bound me in relationship with the omnipotent God. I did not know the depth of God's assignment for me (for my family), until decades after, when its manifestation started unwrapping itself.

My entire life in Lagos state, Nigeria, were all my spiritual baking and grilling moments. None of these experiences did I ever envisaged will swim to my path in life, nor were learned through my parents, nor were read or known from somewhere; except from HIS words which always lightens my heart in most of my miry worlds.

The former part of the above scripture shows me that Jesus had the need to send His disciples out, they had lived with Him, listened to His words, saw Him performing miracles. He equipped the 12 with instructions, into the world of experience that is filled with demonic operations. The question is, why will Jesus send His disciples out into the world He too knew was filled with 'wolves'?

"Behold, I send you out as sheep in the midst of wolves. Therefore, be wise as serpents and harmless as doves." ~
Matthew 10:16

Also,

"These things I have spoken to you, that in Me you may have peace. In the world, you will have tribulation; but be of good cheer, I have overcome the world." ~ *John 16:33*

Worthy to mention was the miry clay of my job search which seemed unending. Every information of job vacancies/openings was followed up with fully packed resume *(curriculum vitae, CV, in Nigeria)* hoping to be called for interview; accompanied with all my prayers and fasting, the expectation to have an end to financial struggles and pressures was held on. The advent of mobile phones was yet undiscovered at that time *(early '90s)*, so I have to set up dates and times to visit the companies for my application status, all to no avail.

A day came, I didn't know if I should call it faithful, when an HR of one of the numerous companies I applied for, gave me an interview date for a client service representative. According to his words,

'I want to do you a favor, I 've been noticing your coming to check your application status. What I need to do is to bring forward your folder and grant you interview.'

Sincerely, this is a position I hated with every fiber in me, because it's a commission paid job, the more of their product you can sell the more your commission. But I don't need to accommodate negative thought in my heart for this 'open door'. Joy filled my being, I felt like throwing a party of 'yoke has been broken' because it's been 3 years into my searching spree.

As expected, the day came, praying and fasting was on the line, with no doubt that I have received the job already. Anyway, I made my presence known to the receptionist, who went inside to let his boss know about my presence. About 30 mins into my sitting at the reception, I started feeling uneasiness, I allowed another 15 mins to roll by, before I went back to ask the receptionist if his boss was aware of any scheduled interview.

His 'no' response did not sink into me but his next statement threw me off balance, *"I thought you are 'ogas'...* His tongue seems glued to his upper mouth at this point, as he couldn't finish his sentence while he stared at me when talking, but I already knew the picture that is about to be unreeled. To confirm this, one after the other, staffs started trickling out in ones and in twos to go home, an indication of end of an office day. I felt like bashing into the cubicle-office area to disgrace him and make other staff hear his after-office hour plans (*I didn't even know which of the cubicles was his, I did not know if I have enough evidence against him to authenticate the assumed plan, above all, I'm just going to put the receptionist in problem*).

I felt so sad, upon all my efforts and expectations of getting out of the financial mess I was, now seemed to engulf me, every step and at every attempt I made. I decided to let the receptionist know that I was nothing to his boss but an ordinary job seeker. We therefore both planned that I am aware of his intention. The receptionist (*my angel, I referred to him later*) went in the office to inform him, in the umpteenth time, of a lady awaiting his attention.

"Oh, I forgot someone was waiting on me. Anyway, I don't want to keep you waiting, while you are leaving tell her to come in."

"But sir, I need to wait, so I can securely lock the door, and drop the key off to the usual place," he retorted.

"Don't worry, I can do all that when I am done." The boss responded to the receptionist.

But as planned, this guy stood around for me, in case something goes against our plans.

As I was ushered into the boss' office, he got up, behind a wooden desk, neck tie, loosened down to chest area, trying to soothingly apologize for the delay, and that it was one of the days his workload was piled up... he was walking towards my standing statute behind a closed door! I knit my back to the door handle, so I will know what to do if he made any attempt to touch me or lock the door. I was poignantly irritated! I see those moves in movies and dramas, not as real as finding myself in it. I knew I must act fast... Sharply I cut in to whatever his epistles were.

"When did I become part of your workload, to be completed after office hour? Is this the way you interview ladies after office hours to defile them? You told me to come for interview at 4:00pm, with an intention to waste my time till after office hours? Did my CV show me as single?" I was talking and screaming at the same time.

He responded rhetorically to me with a 'bone-face' attitude; "Why are you yelling, I've not done anything wrong". By this time, he was at an arm's stretched distance.

"Are you one of the SU's?" (In those days Scripture Union members, especially ladies on campuses are popular called SU's). "That's why you are unemployed..." he commented, while trying to touch me at my upper arm. Before I could feel his nasty fingers on my skin, a sharp thunderous slap landed on his good-for-nothing face. I be-lieved his cheek must have smol-dered under the pressure of my slap. I made sure to balance the smoldering on the second cheek, my heeled shoes helped me to in-fuse groin pressure that forced him to bow for me!

All he could do was to groan while I jerked the door ajar, happy to see the receptionist standing at doorway, who witnessed the scene, and I was very happy to see his secret plan foiled for his subor-dinate to assist me to propagate his wicked intentions, while I left the office.

This is what I called the miry of deception. How many are the la-dies that had been lured or tricked into a fallacy of this kind? Count-less are the ones that fell victims and not offered the job, double trouble. And how many are the ladies that goes around with garment of deceit, defile themselves and polluting the world with evil, all in the guise of job seeking. One thing is sure,

> *"Unless the Lord builds the house, they labor in vain who build it; Unless the Lord guards the city, the watchman stays awake in vain" ~~ Psalm 127:1*

Also, no matter how ignorant you could be, your relationship with God will activate Holy Spirit within you to know some things are not just normal. He will then set some apparatus around you to be in motion of defense. I mean apparatus that will be a way of escape for you, and at the same time bring glory to His name. David says:

> *"Yea, though I walk through the valley of the shadow of death, I will*

fear no evil; For You are with me" ~
(Psalm 23:4)

Your walk with God will ulti-
mately make a way of escape for
you;

"If it had not been the Lord who
was on our side," Let Israel now
say —
"If it had not been the Lord who was
on our side, when men rose up
against us, then they would have
swallowed us alive...Our soul has es-
caped as a bird from the snare of the
fowlers! The snare is broken, and we
have escaped" ~~ Psalm 124:1-3; 7

Relatively, your way of escape
may not be the route you wish; it
might be a route to another route,
to another route, before the destination. Another person's route of
escape could be a sojourn in for-
eign land, like Daniel in bible; it
could take the stop-over shape in

79

fish belly like in Jonah's story. All that matter is that you stay focused onto the Author and Designer of routes. He knows where and when to show up. And anytime He shows up, He is always 'on time'. When you think He is late, that is when His arrival is about taking all the glory to Himself.

Follow me to check out Joseph's journey from pit to palace. You expect the plan of wickedness of the brothers to be foiled and revealed to their father, right? But that was not God's route! You don't expect someone that has such dream to be a victim in Potiphar's house, the scene of life that sent him to many years in prison, right? That's not God's route either. But for him not to lose focus or be deterred with distractions, the Bible says *God was with him*, until he manifested at his destination, the Palace. You will end well in Jesus name. Your Palace experience will not be destroyed before you get there in Jesus name.

So also, in any areas or levels of miry clay we might find ourselves, remember that He that knows you well is always with you. He knows what to do and exactly when to do it.

Anyway, you surely want to know the plight of this HR man and want to know if my angel receptionist was victimized or not. My point is, when God saves you from a miry clay experience, it is love and faithfulness of God in display, you have just enjoyed, you don't attempt to go back, or to visit the miry scene again, it will always be a scary experience for those that had it, not even a passerby like me.

All the lessons and praises therein is what is needed to edify others.

Bear in mind that some could not get out of such miry clay experience, many came out with sharp and deep cut that leaves indelible scars on their souls.

All you need to do is to search out the knowledge from it, and hold fast to the teachings thereof.

How did this miry affect my job search spree? What did I do next? These will unfold in the next Chapter.

Prayers:

- *My Father, my maker, every pit along my destiny, Lord fill it with your supernatural glory.*
- *Peradventure someone has planned or is planning a pit for me and mine, I declare the pit to turn to his grave in the name of Jesus!*

Chapter 5

THE RESCUER CAME

"Even to your old age, I am He, And even to gray hairs I will carry you! I have made, and I will bear; Even I will carry, and will deliver you" ~ Isaiah 46:4

With the best appraisal of my faith practices, I am never a witch-hunter neither am I an advocate of fear when it comes to satanic operations and its devices. While I am not ignorant of 'its' existence and 'its' manipulative tendencies, I also know that my warfare is not canal but you never see my Holy Ghost outburst until this day I had an open confrontation with satanic operation's base.

Going through one of my church's fasting spree, this one involved been at the overnight prayer section, called vigil, scheduled to start at 11pm. I overslept into few minutes before midnight. My husband couldn't go with me because he had to be at work in the morning.

While locking my door and an outer door which oversee the roof of an adjacent building and boys' quarters, I heard some strange sounds. I turned around, and on the center of the boys' quarters and kitchen area were these six cats looking my way, having meeting! I mean it's not strange to see cats around, even on the street, but not six cats looking my way at the same time! At midnight!

With my hand holding a gallon of water and my right hand

gripped tightly to my bible. I spoke to make them see the reason why they need to disperse.

'I am coming, that is my path way, I am made to have dominion over you cats...'

Then, I commanded them with spiritual tongues, to flee. By the time I got off the stairs, closer to where they were, only two remained, steering at me. I dashed forward with my right hand of fire, up with my Bible against the two, with scriptures of the sword of God and heavenly brimstone to overpower and destroy them and their plans. I never knew cats could fly until that midnight, from the ground I saw cats fly, or is that jumping? I saw cats moving from the ground to rooftop!

After 2 weeks, one of the tenants asked, if I knew that our landlady had been terribly sick, came back from hospital 2 days ago. I replied, no. She continued to tell me that they have been warned not to let me know she was sick, because she didn't want me to come to greet her. I asked why should she say that, in order to hear more from her, she shrugged her shoulder.

To give God all the glory for victory He gave me and make public show of the devil. I decided to go visit...

Few hours later, I pretended no one had told me anything, at the same time, I wanted to confirm what she meant with that statement, she needed to confess and let there be witnesses. Few of the tenants saw me going, I really didn't want to enter landlady area anyway, I decided to be talking along her corridor to inform imaginary

person that I wanted to greet landlady. I was almost grabbing her
door knob when her husband came
out to plead that I should go back.
At the same time, there were people downstairs watching, heard
her scream and begging that the
closer I get the heater the flame on
her became.

Anyway, I was not equipped to
know how to lead such wicked
person to the Lord, because my
prayers for her then was to reap the
fruits of her wickedness. I couldn't
lead her to salvation till we moved
out of the house. She avoided me
every time, walks other way anytime she noticed my presence.

This was when yokes were totally broken and doors began to
open. Even when I was still there, I
enjoyed the freshness of God daily.

"Lest Satan should take advantage of us; for we are not ignorant of his devices" ~~ *2 Corinthians 2:11*

When obstacles come one's way, most times it looks blurry to know the next step of direction to take. That is why children of God should always be armored with resources, people, wisdom, talents and gifts that we have earned one way or the other. In as much as we don't know when all these will be needed, obstacles kick in and activate their usefulness at every level of our miry experience.

At my own level, what kicks in for my next life agenda was wisdom. I made a quick decision to stop looking for white collar job; more so, I thought I was new to Lagos State, slow to make new friends; now, married, my quicker ways to move or make connections drastically and culturally reduced, been housed in an unfriendly housing, seemed to be living in a cage.

I started hawking on the road side of shuttle bus garage, where inter-city and inter-state buses gather to discharge and fill up their buses with commuters. This for someone like me, was highly demeaning and sad. But up until now, I never thought of it to be sad, because if God made a way for me from the claws of an 'He-goat' (in previous chapter), whose aim was to dent and abuse me, how won't He make another way out into my next victory.

This is what I always want to leave back on people's minds, **that no one is ever forgotten in the agenda of God. Just wait on Him!**

For me to start somewhere and somehow, I had to approach a close to home company's boss, whom I once applied into for a job, to grant me a space along his company's outer fence, to use for my hawking display. The man felt so concerned and regretted not been able to employ me as staff. Anyway, he granted me the space. I took the offer with glad tidings because of the peace that I had, at least to be going out of the house like any other people that went to daily work or job.

I made a local wooden glass display table for my donuts, to make it neat and untouched for flies. Variety of biscuits (cookies) and soft drinks (called soda) were all I could start with because of the little budget I had.

You know what, it is true that **when you don't despise the days**

of your small beginning, the latter days shall surely, greatly increase. Before I knew it, some mixtures of sympathy, love and empathy turned me to become a 'local champion'.

What I meant with this was, I literally became advocate for some, mentor for some, counsellor for some, mommy for some, big aunt for some...I had more people to rally round me, to make my day filled with pleasantries and be a help for someone.

I graduated from being a donut seller to food seller! I crack some people up with laughter when I tell them this. The reason was, the only gain/profit I had from donut, comes only when I could sell a dozen, the price of two out of twelve donut was my profit! It was so difficult to eat out of it! Very painful to see my girls (children) wanting to have taste of it, but I couldn't afford it! Otherwise I will be eating up profit that's needed to accumulate.

But with selling of food! Whoa, a scoop of rice, few grains of brown beans and pieces of fried plantains, made my day jolly...

God's plan is always sure! My third level of graduation turned me to frozen meat dealer! Oooh... this was the juicy part.

Do not ever look down on your helper, irrespective of their shape, height, color, background or sex. One of my acquaintances stopped over at my stall to ask where I usually purchase the meat for the food that I sell. 'Of course, general market place', I replied. My response was an indication to her that I never heard or knew anything

close to what she was about to dis-
close to me. She shoved out of her
large size Ghana-must-go bag, a
neatly and sizeable packed cow
meat, was swung at me. It looked
so pretty to see how cow meat
could be hygienically packed for
sale! This must be from oversea, I
told her.

Quite unlike what I grew to
know (even till now), sights of
meat selling at local marketplace is
to see batches and sections laid out
or piled on each other in a rectan-
gular shaped wooden box, covered
with thin wooden slab that serves
as the display board; (a dancing
floor for flies of different shapes, to
rejoicing on the red-blooded cow
meat until it turns to light brown),
for buyers to see and negotiate before buying. The thin slab also
serves as the cutting board. Sellers

are often male. The exposure of the meat to the scorching sun of the day, would have half-grilled it before the night time buyers comes around.

Anyway, this lady went to buy this meat "UAC Packed Frozen Meat" for her household consumption. But I went to visit the company to observe, but ended up running into a street neighbor, whose supervisor was someone God made me to help secure an employment at Oyo State government, ministry of education.

Yes, this was one of the events that relate to the word of God

"The lines are fallen to me in pleasant places..." ~ *Psalm 16:6*

Before I knew it, this supervisor led me from one table to another table, filled and signed few documents that authorized me to buy in quantities, rather than in pieces (when I never had prospective buyers or companies to supply to), it all looked as if UAC was expecting my arrival to be an indirect distributor of the frozen packed meat, fully labeled in sizes.

I put together few skills of flyer design, talked to some people for patronage; I went in agreement with few people for references; physical and spiritual efforts earned me two restaurant owners in Victoria Island, Lagos, that maintained regular purchase. Also, my husband's efforts to bring back empty coolers on every Friday from his place of work, made our weekends to be jollier…

Things changed, status and postures changed, our laughter

changed too. Whoa, meals without meat turned to meal with assorted/variety/selected meats. Grilled, Fried and Saucy meat became our evening snack!

When God's time to bless His children comes, there's nothing you can compare its feelings with, you surely going to instantly become 'those who dream'.

But while you are awaiting that lifting from that position of miry, I implore you to be laser focused on only Him and do your portion of the contract – to be obedient; serve and worship Him in truth and in spirit; love yourself at that point, don't throw in towel quickly because He knows you well, sees where you are and knows the best route to take you to. You don't even know if you are being tested, that means, He is watching you!

Keep doing what you know best doing.

More importantly, be faithful in what you think is little, let God have His way all through.

"His Lord said to him, 'Well done, good and faithful servant; you have been faithful over a few things, I will make you ruler over many things. Enter into the joy of your Lord." ~~
Matthew 25:23

Prayer:

• *My Father, my Creator, by Your power, I unlock all doors of my greatness that the enemy has possession of, I take back my possessions, by force in Jesus name.*

• *Oh Lord God my Father, every route to my next level will not be hindered in Jesus name.*

Chapter 6

WAY-MAKER: MY GPS
(God's Plan is Sure)

"Thus, says the Lord, who makes a way in the sea, and a path through the mighty waters… Behold, I will do a new thing, now it shall spring forth; Shall you not know it? I will even make a road in the wilderness, And rivers in the desert"
~ Isaiah 43:16; 19

My household was yet to recover from the dream of becoming 'meat seller', graduated from roadside 'rice and beans' hawker, when my husband came back from work to release the news of a double open door that will relocate the entire family to USA through a program called Diversity Visa Lottery, with the support of a 'brotherly friend' (that is a huge story for some other time).

I was bewildered, joyous and scared at the same time at this news. How this came about was too hard and too much to fathom.

Becoming a supplier of meat was like 6-8 months experience. Prior to this news of relocation, my family was constantly being featured on city and state television news for promotion of a video lottery our daughter (one year old at that time) won. We were already in the public eyes for God's favor when this bigger news came.

God brought the fame from nowhere, He created the way, even when we least expected, and made available all the provisions; He lifted people up for our sake, grace was in abundance for our mental, physical and spiritual needs and availability of money was sufficient for the preparations and eventual relocation to USA. This experience of total victory from miry clay, what God didn't allow to submerge us, was a very deep dream that took me several years to wake out from. Our eventual take off that day was a miracle, flying in an aircraft (that up until that day was only seen on the TV or awed by its beauty when hovering in the sky near my area) seems unbelievable. My close to 20 hours journey was without napping time, talk less of deep sleep. You know why? It's impossible for you to sleep again while you are already in a dreamland!

Several times, I still pinch myself occasionally or ask my husband to be sure if we are in the United States of America. This made

Psalm 126 to be so real to me, and up till now whenever I read that chapter I appreciate the goodness of God in my life. He is the Rewarder of those who diligently seek Him indeed!

The awesomeness of God was so huge that the landlady was just staring at us from the corridor, wishing us well! You know what? The truck we booked for moving our stuffs was returned, our loads became so small that there was nothing to load into the truck because neighbors started trooping in to request and pick ALL our belongings, one after the other, to prayerfully use them as a point of contact, that God, that lifted us up out miry situations will be available for them too. This was very touching for me.

We had no obligation than to go lie flat on God's altar: to proclaim His majesty again and again; to re-dedicate our lives back unto His hands; to lower our guards down at His feet and desire His grace to be made abundant to us in every-thing we do; and above all, that His WILL AND MANDATE will con-tinuously guide us into all truth.

When God started manifesting His hand of grace and faithfulness in our lives and in our ministry, it became obvious that He wanted us to teach and help people who is presently experiencing similar things we had been through, to know that HE the Lord, neither for-sake nor forget anyone. Also, to share with people about the things I did while I was in the middle of miry clay to be the same nuggets that can help them out too. More importantly, the foundation therein is erected in the word of God.

I may not know the depth or nature of your miry experience right now, but let me say this to you, WAIT! That was what I did. I waited, I did not lose faith, I did not condemn myself, I did not indulge in blame game, or point fingers on others or some witch-craft somewhere, nor condemn my God and what He can do:

"I waited patiently for the Lord; And He inclined to me, and heard my cry. He also brought me up out of a horrible pit, out of the miry clay, and set my feet upon a rock, and established my steps" ~ Psalm 40:1

Just wait and see HIS hand lifting you up!

Prayers:

- *My Father, My Maker, I receive the strength to totally wait on you alone.*

- *My Father, my Rock, everything and situation that will make me to be distracted while waiting on you, let it be frustrated.*

Chapter 7

WHAT HE SAYS, HE WILL DO

"For the vision is yet for an appointed time; But at the end it will speak, and it will not lie. Though it tarries, wait for it; Because it will surely come, It will not tarry"

~ Habakkuk 2:3

This chapter is a type of mire we can put ourselves because of choices we make in life. Before I dive deeper into this, I need to reiterate the omnipotent and faithfulness character of God. Indeed, whatever He sets HIS mind on doing, He will do. His purpose can never be withheld by anyone.

I once read the story of two brothers, one promised the

other brother a gift of $10 if he allows him to break 3 eggs on his head. The other brother stared back knowing fully well that his brother wasn't working to have earn such money, and he would have known of any gift of money he ever had. But he reluctantly agreed to the offer because it is a way to have money and at least trusted his brother will make good his promise.

Without wasting time, the brother broke the first egg, and with a lot of ridicule and making fun of this poor brother of his, he broke the second egg after wasting a lot of time.

With the egg yolk dripping down his face, waiting impatiently as he awaits the prolonged jest ordeal to be over, the brother with $10 promise ran out! Bewildered and feeling shortchanged', his head still covered with the two eggs, he screamed, "Come back, it's not yet three! Come and smash the third egg, so I can clean up quickly".

His brother replied, "No! I am not going to do the third egg because I can't afford to give the $10..."

Just like this story, the world is filled with unfulfilled and broken promises, vows, pledges that defiles trust, hope and aspirations, from friends, family members, jobs, contracts, and the list is unending.

The Almighty God is not like human, what He says He will do, He does. All of our efforts to run away from His course only compounds and brings struggle to the wheels of our progress.

I stated in chapter 1 how God helped me to peep into my future through dreams. Some of these dreams were forgotten until they become reality. Others were re-membered and I tried to avoid or helped God to modernize their ful-fillment.

One of these second category was the dream about my choice of spouse and ministry assignment. When I was becoming of age to get a date, I detested having friendship with any 'church brother'. Once I sensed any of the so-called broth-ers trying to get close unneces-sarily, always beaming with smiles towards me and want constant conversation, I quickly erect a wall of 'no-go-area'. The reason was that, I don't want to end up becom-ing 'a Pastor's wife'.

During those days, late 70's to early 80's, I personally don't like the appearance of pastors – shabby and oversized high shoulder padded suits. Their shoes are often black, dusty and wacked. Their ties are never congruent with the suit. It appears some of them had the erroneous belief that looking unkempt is synonymous with righteousness. So, while I was serving as a member in ushering and intercessory groups, I avoided the so called 'brothers' like a plague! Coupled with the appearance of these pastors, I realized that their wives don't wear jewelries and even though I grew up in a denomination that look down on people that wears jewelries, no matter how tiny the jewelries may appear. I was never a jewelry freak, but I had about two or three jewelries that were of best quality, and

was not ready to trade them to becoming a pastor's wife.

But when the hand of God "that
is not too short" was ready to pre-
pare me for His specific assignment, He first took the desire to
use jewelry from me. On three occasions, I challenged God concern-
ing this, until He invited me into a
covenant walk with Him. The Lord
said I should always challenge and
remind Him of this covenant
whenever I am confronted with
difficulty in my journey. I have
used this on several occasions and
I still do, and it has brought tre-
mendous blessing into my life and
family because He is a covenant
keeping God.

Also, all the fences and walls I
thought were built against 'brothers' totally fell and crumbled when
my husband that was once fenced

off came back with his proposal! Little did I realized his birth stories were covenanted and wrapped around living in mission house with Church Pastor, like that of Hannah giving up her son, Samuel, to live with Prophet Eli; and working for God. This was what my mother-in-law did to redeem her covenant with God.

In as much as it is imperative for us to have choices, it is also advantageous to allow God's hands to propel His designs to roll around our choices, for our dreams to come into actualization. It was after I learnt to totally release my life to what I called GPS - **God's Plan is Sure**, that the peace and courage to dream again welled up from my inside.

God's faithfulness and mercy are immeasurable when it comes to kingdom assignments. You will think that the way God was faithful with me and my family should be enough catalyst to fuel and propel us into starting the work of the ministry immediately we landed on USA soil. Not so much! We not only dragged to take His assignment fully but we weren't even ready to do 'church ministry'. We were fully serving God in our utmost capacity, but thinking of our haves and have-not.

Analyzing and critiquing our personality as not qualified to start a church, made us to avoid the responsibility.

Our first church point of worship in Newark (New Jersey) made every effort for us to start a branch of the church when we relocated to Ohio but to no avail. All attempts to pioneer a branch of CAC

WOSEM, originally in Nigeria and led by Daddy, Pastor T.O. Obadare (of blessed memory) were also turned down because we thought we were too young to dive into any bureaucratic religious set-up.

A 'release' from the home church we were attending in Ohio gave us an opportunity to start fellowshipping with an American Church where we thought the environment didn't know us, and especially because of the size of the congregation coupled with the fact that it is predominantly 95 percent Caucasian. Now we are completely "free", so we thought.

"Where can I go from Your Spirit? Or where can I flee from Your presence? If I ascend into heaven, You, are there; If I make my bed in hell, behold, You, are there. If I take the wings of the morning, and dwell

in the uttermost parts of the sea, even there Your hand shall lead me...."
Psalm 139:7-12

Alas, if it is not the will of God, it cannot be the way for God. It was while in this American church that God reiterated His covenant, released His word and the commandment to harvest souls into His kingdom came.

There's no amount of strength you think you possess to run away from God's plan that can discourage God from making sure His word come to pass. Pastor Jonah will attest to that because he did a lot of running away from God but eventually was forced to carry out God's mandate (See Jonah 1 - 4).

We also thought we could exchange God's purpose with other type of ministry work.

I looked back to see what people call 'opportunity' to start a ministry, it was never an opportunity for someone like me, not even something I wanted but had no choice than to release myself to what God says He will do, which no logic can interfere with.

Many at times we want to struggle with God's agenda, we want to play smart and play safe, assuring ourselves that God is merciful and He understands. That is correct about our heavenly Father, but I will strongly advice that we should always check back with back with HIM for directions. Even when you think you are unprepared for His tasks and assignment, like Moses, Gideon, Jeremiah and hosts of others, feel free to express your mind (which He sees anyway). I can assure you that His response will be a soothing procedure to go through and overcome, rather than running around and, or remain in the miry of life.

Whoa, I avoided having a church brother as a date, blocked my to-be husband from coming closer for few years, turned down requests or proposals of starting a church three times with excuse that our personalities are not church planter... But today, the miry status is overtaken, I am victorious, moving higher with great strides. To Him be the glory.

Surely, what He says He will do, He will do. His faithfulness is for evermore.

"God is not a man, that He should lie, nor a son of man, that He should repent. Has He said and He will not do? Or has He spoke, and He will not? ~~ Numbers 23:19

Prayers:

- *My Father, my Maker, I cling unto you Lord, let your purpose manifest in my life in Jesus name.*
- *My Father, my Lord, because of your word, restore back to me, all the years the swarming locust, cankerworm, and palmerworm and caterpillar has eaten in Jesus name.*

ABOUT THE AUTHOR

Bosede Adetunji is a Life, Spiritual, and Leadership Coach, Pastor & Motivational Speaker. She was coached and certified under the direct leadership of the legendary John C. Maxwell. Bosede equips individuals and organizations with practical tools that enable them to break barriers, maximize their abilities, and amplify their success throughout all walks of life.

Many lives have been positively impacted because of her leadership and mentoring programs. Testaments of improved relationships, restored marriages, rejuvenated confidence and an overall awareness of self-worth and beauty have been shared by women across the world. Some of her experiences stems from the leadership of Christ Harvest Church, The Esteemed Woman©, and Lily in His Hands© organizations. Bosede currently resides in Houston Texas, and is happily married with children.

DO YOU WANT TO BRING OUT THE LEADER IN YOU?

For more information Visit

http://www.johncmax-
wellgroup.com/bosedeadetunji/
www.lilyinhishands.com
www.bosedeadetunji.com

John Maxwell & Bosede Adetunji

AN INDEPENDENT CERTIFIED
COACH, TEACHER AND SPEAKER
WITH THE JOHN MAXWELL TEAM

The JOHN MAXWELL Team

<u>NOTES</u>

www.ingramcontent.com/pod-product-compliance
Lightning Source LLC
LaVergne TN
LVHW021521080426
835509LV00018B/2600